BRUNO MARS

Publisher and Creative Director: Nick Wells
Project Editor: Polly Prior
Picture Research: Emma Chafer and Polly Prior
Art Director and Layout Design: Mike Spender
Layout Design: Jane Ashley
Digital Design and Production: Chris Herbert

Special thanks to: Emma Chafer, Esme Chapman and Anna Groves

FLAME TREE PUBLISHING
Crabtree Hall, Crabtree Lane
Fulham, London SW6 6TY
United Kingdom
www.flametreepublishing.com

Website for this book: www.flametreepop.com

First published 2013

13 15 17 16 14
1 3 5 7 9 10 8 6 4 2

ISBN 978-0-85775-875-0

Printed in China

BRUNO MARS

UNOFFICIAL

Alice Hudson
Foreword by Lindsay Foley

**FLAME TREE
PUBLISHING**

Contents

Foreword

We've all heard what they say about good things coming in small packages, but Bruno Mars really is the sparkly little diamond you've spent months eyeing up in the shop window. At only 5 ft 5 in, that cheeky-faced exterior might look fairly unassuming, but it tells nothing of the singer who has seamlessly swept onto the scene and put pop music right back on the map.

Average isn't a word I'd ever associate with Bruno and having proved his talent writing hit after hit, it's hard to deny that something pretty special happens when he steps on stage. But aside from two internationally acclaimed albums and the pile of awards cluttering up his mantelpiece and probably his downstairs loo, what's really interesting is that nothing he's done has ever been handed to him on a plate.

In fact everything Bruno has achieved is something he's worked his socks off for and as this book will tell you, nothing - from his humble beginnings to the tabloid headlines – can hold him or his twinkling and infectious brand of pop music from topping the charts.

His star power is undeniable; mesmerising on stage, that irresistible charm has had the best of us swooning down to the tips of our toes and if you can watch the video for 'Just The Way You Are' without melting from the inside out, you are a better person than me. Best have another listen as we get started reading though, just in case...

Lindsay Foley
Weekend Editor, sugarscape.com

Something About the Boy

In 2009, Bruno Mars appeared to arrive suddenly and from nowhere. By the latter part of the following year, the Hawaiian-born singer was absolutely *everywhere*. Turn on the radio and you'd be sure to hear his crooning, velvety vocals; switch on MTV and there he was, fedora-clad, strumming a guitar as he sang. Change channels and … waddaya know? There he was again, same hat, grooving away to a totally different chart-topping beat.

Mr Popularity

At the time of writing, Bruno Mars has sold more than 8 million albums and over 58 million singles worldwide. He'll sell a lot more. He's picked up a host of accolades, including a Grammy and a BRIT. His tracks have been viewed by YouTube users well over a billion times. Bruno was named as the top digital artist of 2011. 'Just the Way You Are' and 'Grenade', the first two singles from his platinum debut album, *Doo-Wops & Hooligans* (2010) were the two most downloaded tracks of that year.

Unorthodox Jukebox (2012), Bruno's sophomore effort, eclipsed the success of *Doo-Wops*. Bruno's first US No. 1 album saw the singer's fame and fortune continue to rise. He may not be a 'Billionaire' just yet but estimates put his net worth at around $15 million and rising fast.

'Be in control. Know who you are. And don't try to be different just to be different.'

Bruno Mars

Timing Is Everything

Four years ago Bruno was officially unsigned – a struggling artist forced to earn his daily bread in the studio, writing hit songs for others to perform. His break came when he was featured on the vocal tracks and in the music videos of two of the year's hit songs – 'Nothin' On You' by B.o.B and 'Billionaire' by Travie McCoy. Bruno co-wrote the songs. These songs launched him into public view and earshot; and the public, it soon transpired, loved Bruno and wanted more. The timing couldn't have been better as Atlantic Records got his first album out to build on the growing buzz about Bruno.

A Hard-Working Boy

Bruno is a fan of hard work, as it's got him to where he is today. 'As a child he could never get enough practice time,' his dad says. Bruno's jivin' and lip-curlin' routines as Little Elvis were what he lived for. Practising was work yet it was also fun.

As a member of a musical clan, little Bruno even did media interviews. Clips of him fielding questions like a pro can be found on YouTube. This early training was invaluable when the boy decided to pursue music as a career. He already knew something about the hard graft and tireless practice that lay ahead.

'I've listened to doo-wop my whole life and I think that's where my writing style comes from … it's very straight and to the point.'

Bruno Mars

'Bruno was always so confident, independent, really strong-willed and kind of a brute – hence the name Bruno, and it kind of just stuck.'

Bruno Mars' sister Jamie Hernandez

Mr Popularity

Almost certainly due to the eclectic nature of his biggest hits, Bruno's fanbase includes a broad range, from the throngs of teenaged girls to the huge Aussie rugby players he was once mobbed by in an airport. He was quick to be dubbed a 'heart throb' with his baby-faced looks and heart-melting lyrics. Bruno's mixed heritage means different groups of fans around the world can rightfully stake a claim to him.

Talented Trio

Aged just 18, Bruno Hernandez achieved a major coup when he signed a deal with *Motown Records.* However the label lost interest and quietly dropped him. Although Bruno says now that being dropped by his label was 'a reality check' and 'the best thing that ever happened to me', the singer faced an uncertain future at the time.

One lasting legacy of his brief time with Motown was meeting songwriter Philip Lawrence. Together with Ari Levine, a producer with his own basic studio, the friends formed the production outfit The Smeezingtons in 2008 and were soon offered money for a song. At first Bruno, still the aspiring performer, resisted but he eventually agreed to sell.

When people fall is when they're like: "Ok. Now I'm here, what's next? A clothing line?" That's not what I'm trying to do.'

Bruno Mars

Singing From His Own Songsheet

The first big success with all three Smeezingtons was 'Get Sexy' by UK girl group, the Sugababes. In the UK, it peaked at No. 2 and sold 165,000 copies. The trio continued to pen tunes for other artists, Mars holding onto his dream of solo success, just putting it temporarily to one side.

Diverse hits by The Smeezingtons include Cee Lo Green's 'Forget You', Brandy's 'Long Distance', Far East Movement's 'Rocketeer' and the theme song from the 2010 Vancouver Winter Olympics, 'Wavin' Flag', by K'Naan.

'Bruno is just doing his thing and it's awesome to see … he's definitely gonna take over the world … he is killing it, he is a human jukebox.'

Travie McCoy

Nothin' On You

Bruno had officially signed to Atlantic Records in 2009. It was when a couple of his label mates given Smeezington-produced music decided to keep Bruno's vocals that the public started to hear the man as well as his music. The timing couldn't have been more perfect. 'Nothin' On You' by B.o.B and Travie McCoy's 'Billionaire' were both created during the same week over the summer of 2009 and released only a month apart in 2010 – B.o.B's in February and Travie McCoy's in March.

The tracks featuring Bruno performed well: 'Nothin' On You' reaching the top in the key US and UK markets. It meant Bruno and his team were just a few savvy business decisions away from launching the singer into the pop stratosphere. The May 2010 release of a four-track digital-only EP, titled *It's Better If You Don't Understand* was a great way to keep the buzz about Bruno going or, as Atlantic Records' John Janick put it, 'to ensure people knew he was a "real" artist'.

'You just gotta believe in yourself and keep doing what you're doing. I know it sounds cheesy but that's the truth.'

Bruno Mars

'For me to keep wanting to do music,
I need to be excited about what's happening. . . .
I have a short attention span.'
Bruno Mars

Laid-Back Groover

In the second half of 2010, Bruno's career suddenly gained momentum and by 2011, was hurtling at top speed. That year Atlantic decided on an October release for *Doo-Wops & Hooligans,* Bruno's first full-length album. Tracks released prior to the launch were the critically acclaimed 'The Other Side' featuring Cee Lo Green and B.o.B, the love ballad 'Just The Way You Are' (both in July 2010) and the anthem-like lament, 'Grenade' (September 2010).

Doo-Wops proved Bruno had 'made it'. The album debuted at No. 3 on the *Billboard* Hot 200 – shifting 55,000 units in the first week. The No. 1 singles 'Just The Way You Are' and 'Grenade' even featured in the Top 10 of the *Billboard* Hot 100 at the same time, even though they were released months apart. Another track from the album, 'The Lazy Song', scored his third consecutive UK No. 1. *Doo-Wops* attracted mainly positive reviews though some critics viewed it as an overly commercial attempt to appeal to everyone.

Beach Boy

Bruno Mars was born into a large, musical family in tropical, laid-back Hawaii on 8 October 1985. His birth certificate records the name Peter Gene Hernandez, though the singer claims he's never, ever been called Peter, not since the day his dad decided his chubby-cheeked toddler resembled the famous wrestler, Bruno Sammartino.

Born Into Music

Little Bruno is blessed with culturally diverse and musical genes. Father Peter Hernandez, a Latin percussionist from New York, is half Puerto Rican, with Jewish relatives. Mother Bernadette 'Bernie' San Pedro was born in the Philippines, with Spanish roots. A professional singer and hula dancer who met Bruno's father while they were performing in the same show, Bernie tragically suffered a brain aneurysm and died aged 55 on 1 June 2013, just three weeks before the scheduled start of Bruno's Moonshine Jungle Tour.

Bruno's father ran a Las Vegas-style 1950s revue show five nights a week in Waikiki, the Honolulu neighbourhood in which Bruno grew up. It featured the family band, The Love Notes performing Motown hits and doo-wop medleys. When Bruno was four years old he was allowed to join in, and began to perform five nights a week. He became an instant hit and even enjoyed 15 minutes of early fame as 'The World's Youngest Elvis Impersonator'.

'It was like turning into Batman … you put on a sequined jumpsuit and all of a sudden you're Bruno, the world's youngest Elvis impersonator.'

Bruno Mars on his early performances

It's All About The Music

Bruno attended President Theodore Roosevelt High School in Hawaii and soaked up the sun and the reggae-infused vibe, and all throughout his school days remained focused on music and performing. He was in a reggae band and at one stage performed a revue show with friends in a similar vein to the Love Notes.

Bruno's ears were constantly filled with Motown and Elvis, and the 1950s doo-wop he's always loved. Rock 'n' roll, gospel, reggae, hip-hop, R&B and pop were other musical genres Bruno listened to growing up. Just because he loved 1950s and 1960s music didn't mean the young Bruno wouldn't open his ears to other, more modern sounds. In fact the eclectic mix of music enjoyed by Bruno as he was growing up goes a long way to explain his genre-hopping style as a recording artist today. In the early days of his career, his gigs would often include bits by, and even full covers of, other artists, for instance singing Nirvana's 'Teen Spirit' over Michael Jackson's 'Billie Jean'.

According to Bruno, a piece of music that's truly inspiring is more than just a song – it's an event. He cites Queen's epic 'Bohemian Rhapsody'. 'I'm sure that shocked the world, that song,' he told *GQ* magazine.

More Than A Voice

With his songwriting skills and production mastery resulting in a string of hits – both for himself and for other artists – Bruno is a far cry from the manufactured pop star commonly found in today's *X Factor* influenced recording industry. He's a skilled pianist, guitarist and drummer, though Bruno himself claims he is 'not great' at any of these instruments. Yet his wide range of musical skills – not to mention learned professionalism and the ability to work in just about any musical style and song format from rap to soul, rock, reggae and disco – has undeniably helped to boost the 27-year-old's credibility.

'Groove is very important … even in ballads there has to be some kind of tempo and some kind of movement.'

Bruno Mars

'Growing up performing – that was normal for me. Everyone in my family sings, plays instruments. It's what we do.'

Bruno Mars

Get Up And Dance

Performing is Bruno's greatest strength. It's also the aspect of his career he loves most. He wants people to dance, to sing along and party with him at his gigs. Nowhere has this been more evident for the world to see than during his live, televised performances at the Grammys. In 2012, it was a rendition of 'Runaway Baby' while in 2013, along with fellow superstars Rihanna and Sting, he wowed with a reggae-tinged Bob Marley tribute.

Maybe it's down to all the practice he got performing Elvis routines in the family show as a kid, maybe it's his excellent work ethic; or it could simply be that Bruno Mars is a natural-born performer, one of those rare talents destined for a life on stage? When you see Bruno perform live, it's highly likely you will lean towards the last theory. Even those who dislike his music are often won over when they see the star in concert.

'It took me a while to finally get it,

but when I got it, I think I got it right.

And I'm very proud of how my songs are

representing me as an artist.'

Bruno Mars

'I'm Bruno Mars. Get ready to hold your face 'cos I'm about to blow it off.'

Bruno Mars

Hooligans

The 'treat' is his backing band, The Hooligans. True to the bygone era of doo-wop music of which Bruno is such a fan, according to Bruno there's nothing better than jamming with his band on stage. The eight-piece features brass instruments like the saxophone and trumpet, as well as plenty of keys, drums and bass. Members include best mate Phil Lawrence from The Smeezingtons on backing vocals and his older brother Eric on drums. The enjoyment of the performers is always evident at every show says Bruno.

'I hear some screams and I laugh to myself. I always get a kick out of it. I'm three feet tall, basically. What the hell are you girls screaming at?'

Bruno Mars

He's Got The Look

Bruno's public image is as accessible as his music, but he's still an individual with his own style. His retro look has been further customized with various tattoos: his mother's name on his shoulder, an anchor on his right forearm and a gypsy lady (for good luck) on his left forearm. He can pull off old school suit pants, fancy jackets or a tuxedo as easily as he rocks skinny trousers and denim or a leather jacket. It's the headgear though that's most synonymous with his style. The singer's hat habit originated from the loss of his afro, when he decided to get rid of it after high school.

Bruno's appearance on the cover of *Playboy*'s annual 'Sex and Music' edition in 2012 – the 165-cm star cosying up to long-legged model and Miss April, Raquel Pomplun – saw the star go down in lad-mag history as only the tenth male ever to feature on *Playboy*'s cover. An honour and a nod of appreciation not only for Bruno's music but for his sexy, cool image too – effortlessly cool.

'With my being from Hawaii and being very family-oriented I don't really have a fear of a tragic ending. I don't see any tragic ending for me.'

Bruno Mars

International Treasure

Following the success of *Doo-Wops & Hooligans* Bruno could have been forgiven for 'playing it safe' on his next album – but that's just not his style. Sophomore albums are always subject to harsher levels of scrutiny from critics and fans alike. Could Bruno live up to the pressure and deliver something truly 'out of this world'? The success of *Doo-Wops* was always going to be difficult to beat.

> '*If I was a billionaire, I'd have a diamond encrusted hat, made of unicorn fur. Why? Do you have a diamond-encrusted hat, made of unicorn fur?*'
>
> Bruno Mars

A Different Direction

Unorthodox Jukebox was eventually released on 11 December 2012 amid an almost deafening buzz. Bruno wrote most of the tracks while touring and promoting *Doo-Wops*. He was able to listen to lots of different music in different cities around the world, and was keen to take a new direction in his writing and to incorporate all the best elements of what he heard.

As well as his Smeezingtons buddies, Bruno worked with big-name producers on the album, including Mark Ronson and Diplo. Featuring 10 tracks, the album has elements of disco and funk as well as soul, rock, pop, R&B and hip-hop. Damien Marley features, lending his vocals to the reggae-inspired 'Liquor Store Blues'.

Chart Topper

Unorthodox Jukebox rewarded Bruno with his first No. 1 album in the States. In its first week, it sold over 187,000 copies. Power ballad 'Locked Out Of Heaven', the album's lead single, spent six consecutive weeks at No. 1 on the *Billboard* Hot 100. *Jukebox*'s second single, musing ballad 'When I Was Your Man', was a smash hit too, also reaching the top of the *Billboard* Hot 100 and making the Top 10 in 15 countries.

Jukebox was generally well received, although criticisms of Bruno's refusal to 'pick a lane' musically were repeated, while his lyrics were deemed perfunctory, bland, crude or uninspired by some. For his part, Bruno remained unapologetic about the eclectic nature of the work, or any of his work for that matter.

'Music is not math. It's science. You keep mixing the stuff up until it blows up on you, or it becomes this incredible potion.'

Bruno Mars

'I feel it's my job to continue being a student of music if I want to continue being an artist and a producer of other artists. You have to keep filling your mind with other music. You have to be ahead of the curve.'

Bruno Mars

Ultimate Dream

By May 2013, *Unorthodox Jukebox* had clocked up international sales of well over a million. It was time for Bruno to hit the road with his eight-piece backing band. Spanning 26 countries over a 10-month period, Bruno's Moonshine Jungle Tour was originally scheduled to include 45 North American shows and 31 in the United Kingdom and Europe. Tickets sold like hot cakes, however, with all UK concerts selling out. The demand saw Bruno announce four additional UK dates, including an extra night at London's 20,000-capacity O2 Arena. With Moonshine, Bruno is finally, joyfully, living out his ultimate dream.

As well as being a sell-out, No. 1 artist, Bruno is also known to support various charities, including Musicians on Call, Red Cross, DoSomething and Candie's Foundation. Despite his laid-back nature and the chilled-out, easy-going vibes he projects, underneath Bruno's relaxed exterior is an ambitious individual with a clear vision – to keep honing his skills and making music – for the long haul.

Star Of The Screen

It's obvious that Bruno is comfortable on stage. Still, his decision to let producers of hit show *Saturday Night Live* talk him into not only appearing and performing live but also hosting the entire show was a brave one. 'I've never done comedy before, I've never acted before', he later joked. This edition of *Saturday Night Live* attracted millions of viewers. He left the audience in stitches with his jokes and comedic skits, in which he imitated Justin Bieber and Katy Perry.

Mars was a contributor to one of the most popular teen-movie franchises of recent years with the track 'It Will Rain', which featured on the soundtrack for *The Twilight Saga: Breaking Dawn Part 1*. It was his 11th Top 10 single. Bruno has clocked up an impressive number of TV appearances. He's appeared on *American Idol* and *The X Factor* as well as *The X Factor* final in France.

'I'm not trying to be a circus act. I listen to a lot of music and I want to have the freedom and luxury to walk into a studio and say, "Today I want to do a hip-hop, R&B, soul or rock record."'

Bruno Mars

'Mars' songs connect to our common elements of humanity. Love, acceptance, loss. The ability to marry those sentiments to engaging melodies is what makes his appeal so broad.'

Andrea Ganis, Executive VP, Atlantic Records

Public Mask, Private Face

Bruno Mars is a musician of the twenty-first century. So it's no surprise to find Bruno knows how to work show business in the digital age as well as any other successful pop starlet today. He's active on social media and has Twitter, Facebook and MySpace accounts. Bruno's well aware of the importance of the media rigmarole that is part of the job and regularly posts videos to help him connect with the fans.

Depite the harsh glare of the media spotlight and constant attention from photographers, Bruno manages to come across as open, without giving too much away. He rarely mentions his relationship with model and dancer Jessica Caban. Bruno has admitted the song 'When I Was Your Man' from *Unorthodox Jukebox* was written for Jessica, at a time when he realized he'd not paid enough attention to the relationship and was in danger of losing her. He and Jessica now live together in his $3 million Hollywood home.

Monumental Slip-Up

On 19 September 2010, Bruno was busted while in a casino bathroom for cocaine possession. The singer was arrested and his mug shot taken, in which he was somewhat inappropriately smiling. He immediately apologized and the case was dismissed due to his willingness to take a drug-education course, complete 200 hours of community service and cough up a $2000 fine.

Coconuts On The Beach

Music is Bruno's life: 'It's all I know.' While he told *GQ* that he expects he will one day return to Hawaii with its laid-back aloha spirit to retire 'on a beach, drinking out of a coconut, watching some kids running around in the sand, looking at the ocean'; performing remains a part of that vision.

'People haven't seen nothing.
They don't even know what
I'm about to do and that's what
I can't wait to show the world.'

Bruno Mars

Bruno Mars Vital Info

Birth Name	Peter Gene Hernandez
Birth Date	8 October 1985
Birth Place	Honolulu, Hawaii, US
Nationality	American
Height	1.65 m (5 ft 5 in)
Hair Colour	Brown
Eye Colour	Brown

Online

brunomars.com:	Bruno's official website packed with info about tour dates and music releases
twitter.com/BrunoMars:	Join millions of others and follow Twitter updates from the man himself @BrunoMars
facebook.com/thatbrunomars:	Read what Bruno Mars has to say on his Facebook page
youtube.com/artist/bruno-mars:	Mars-ter all Bruno's lyrics on his official YouTube channel
myspace.com/brunomars:	Listen to and watch everything Bruno Mars related
flametreepop.com:	Celebrity, fashion and pop news, with loads of links, downloads and free stuff!

Acknowledgements

Alice Hudson (Author)

From New Zealand, Alice fused twin passions for writing and music while a student, reviewing and interviewing international bands and DJs. She spent five years writing for Kiwi news outlets including the *NZHerald,* followed by a four-year stint in London, where she worked as a financial media researcher and analyst, press officer, and online editor. She began freelancing in 2012 and currently splits her time between New Zealand and the UK.

Lindsay Foley (Foreword)

Lindsay Foley is an entertainment journalist, who works heavily across celeb gossip and music as Weekend Editor for Sugarscape.com. She spends a large amount of her time on the red carpet, engaged in serious activities that include blindfolding popstars and persuading boybands to read aloud from 50 Shades of Grey. It's a hard job, but she supposes someone has to do it.

Picture Credits

All images © **Getty Images**: FilmMagic: 10, 15, 16, 34; Getty Images Entertainment: 1, 3, 7, 8, 18, 22, 26, 28, 31, 39, 44, 46; Getty Images for EIF: front cover & 32; Redferns via Getty Images: 12, 25; WireImage: 21 & back cover, 40, 43.